THE PURPOSE OF PURPOSE

Rod McKenzie, Jr.

For ordering large quantities, please contact the publisher at the following address.

Zovations, Inc.
Email: info@zovations.com
Website: http://www.RodMcKenzieJr.com

First Edition, 2016.

Printed in the United States of America.

Throughout my life, I have been attracted to principles
and teachings that make sense of life.

I want to thank all those who have taken the
initiative to discover, create, and articulate their
knowledge, understanding, and insights.

I know what it takes to try and make sense
of the world. I applaud and appreciate
their efforts from the depths of my soul.

Connect with Rod

Website: www.RodMcKenzieJr.com
Facebook: www.Facebook.com/RodMcKenzieJr
LinkedIn: www.LinkedIn.com/in/RodMcKenzieJr

Thanks for Your Help

I was able to write the first draft of my book in less than three days. A high thanks to the group Tears for Fears for providing my writing soundtrack. It's music that speaks to me, helps me think, and brings peace and understanding to my mind.

Preface

What happens when you sit down to write a book and the first draft is done in less than three days?

I feel very inspired to have been able to write this book. I believe that if we choose to live by having our purpose guide and direct our lives, we will find true happiness.

Over the past five years, my family has encountered some fairly dramatic health hardships.

It seems as though we are finally coming through those challenges, and I am looking forward to the opportunity to help others.

When several of my family members were very sick and the doctors did not know what was causing their problems, I reached the end of my rope.

Through prayer, I was led to the people who could help me help my family.

They led us through several years of recovery and have literally saved the lives of several members of my family.

These individuals have a purpose to help people in unique ways. With their passion, they were able to make a difference in the lives of my family and also in the lives of many others.

They inspire me, and have helped me overcome my health challenges so I can share my knowledge with others.

I am not mentioning their names, but I do want you to know that there are people out there who care, and who will help you overcome your challenges because that is their purpose.

Thank you for saving my family with your purpose-filled lives.

~ Rod McKenzie, Jr.

Contents

When you meet her, you realize just how much joy
she has within her soul. My wife is the most amazing
woman on the planet and has once again
supported me in writing a book.

She is my much better half, and I am
a much better man for having found her years ago.

This book is for you Sweetheart.

Thanks Liz!

Introduction

The first chapter of my book "Are You Ready to Start a Business?" was about how business people sometimes make the big mistake of not knowing why they are starting a business.

I proceeded to explain how if you don't know why you are starting a business, when the going gets tough, you will bolt out of there and your business will fail.

I have become consumed by the entire process of discovering purpose in people's lives, in their businesses, and in just about every aspect of their life.

As I have studied, I have discovered many things and five of them are listed here:

First, many people think they know what their purpose is here on this earth, but they can't quite put it into words.

Second, many people are very intrigued about the prospect of learning what their purpose is.

Third, people don't realize how important the happy experiences they have had in their lives are to their being.

Fourth, people don't realize how important knowing their purpose is to their everyday lives.

Fifth, many people get very emotional when I help them define their purpose into a clear and concise statement.

As I have trained people for years in starting and growing businesses, I have discovered that people are very willing to learn, if the subject applies directly to them.

I began to formulate an idea for a book that would help people discover their own purpose. I wanted to help people understand the value of knowing their purpose in a clear and concise statement. The challenge was how to present the information to make it simple to understand, and yet be a very deep and emotional experience which could change someone's life like it has mine and others.

Inside this book, I will take you on a journey to discover the purpose of purpose. In other words, why you need to know your purpose and what it can do for you.

We will start by understanding what a purpose is and how it will help you in your decision making, how knowing your purpose affects all aspects of your life, and what it means to live a purpose first life.

You will then be taken through an extensive exercise to help you define your purpose in a very clear and concise way.

We will then proceed to help you understand how to live a purpose-filled life by asking questions, finding passion, and discovering how your defined purpose can help you in your personal and professional life.

I really want you to find happiness in all parts of your life. That is why I wrote this book, to bring a smile to your face.

You see, my purpose is: "I thrive when I look at someone smile and know that I contributed to it."

I hope you find this book worth your time and effort. I hope it makes you think, and think hard, about how your life can change and be better than where you are now.

I want you to experience the joy of finding happiness through memories of all the happy times in your life.

I want you to take hold of who you are and what you are about, so you can make a difference in other's lives.

Above all, I want you to smile and share your success with others.

I hope you enjoy the journey with me of finding what your real purpose in life is and how it can bring you real happiness.

The Purpose of Purpose

Chapter 1

What is Purpose?

Purpose is a word that is used to mean many different things, most commonly "why something is done." Why does it matter why we do something or why we do anything at all? If we do something, we do it. Right? We make a decision, and just do something. Why is having a purpose to do something so important?

The answer is that purpose does matter. It's how we are made. We think about what we do and we make decisions based on our knowledge, feelings, thoughts, previous experiences, and even our passions. Our purpose is our motive for doing something. A life without motive is hardly a life worth living.

For as long as people have been alive, their purpose or "why" has almost exclusively outweighed any other reason for doing something.

Take, for example, when you choose to accept a job. At first glance, most people take jobs to make income. But when you take a deeper look, often there is a much stronger purpose for taking a specific job. That purpose can be to do something you know you are good at and be rewarded financially for your efforts and knowledge. For people who have a passion for their job, their purpose is in harmony with what the position requires, and they are able to wake up every morning and go to a place of joy instead of just a job.

Look at sporting events and the fans who attend them. Each team has people who are purposefully engaged harmoniously in cheering and rooting for their team, while at the same time hoping that the other team will fail.

What about when you find someone to commit your life to? The primary reason people are able to have deep relationships is because their purposes are in harmony with each other.

The challenge we then face is knowing how to live our lives with purpose in everything we do. Is it possible? Is it feasible? Is it even a good idea?

The answer is yes. You can do everything in life with purpose, and the results are amazing when you do.

Knowing Your Own Purpose (Your Why)

A personal purpose or "why" is critical to understanding yourself. You need to find out what makes you tick, what drives you, and what it is that makes you want to get out of bed in the morning.

It is knowing their purpose or "why" that enables people to have different levels of success.

Purpose explains why two athletes with similar training and opportunities have such different achievements.

Purpose explains how one person who didn't make a high school team becomes one of the best basketball players in history.

Purpose explains how someone who grew up in poverty can break out of the stereotype and become a business success while so many others fail.

How valuable is knowing your purpose in a relationship? When you meet someone, can you identify if they know who they are and why they are? How long does it usually take to see the confidence and surety come through their persona?

When you have a friend who is always complaining that they don't know what they are doing with their life, how does it make you feel?

What if you are that friend? What if you don't know what you want to do with your life, and you are constantly complaining to others? What if you are constantly complaining to yourself?

A lack of purpose is one of the key contributors to many different types of depression, stress, anxiety, lack of confidence, poor attitude, real unhappiness, lack of hope, and many other things which cause real emotional trauma within a person.

On the other hand, when you find someone who knows their purpose in life, you can see it in them. You can even feel the energy of their confidence. You see how they are guided and directed to do things where they can make a real difference. They often have a magnetic personality where people are drawn to them and want to be around them. When they come into a room, people feel it. Others who have defined their purpose are quiet, but very assured.

The bottom line is, if you have a defined purpose in life, you know who you are and people can tell. Knowing your purpose on the earth is critical to your happiness.

Purpose is Individual

So if a purpose is so critical to happiness, can you find a statement somewhere and just adopt it? Do you have to really do any soul searching to find it, or can you just take something that you really identify with and make it your own?

Well, each one of us on this planet is unique. There are not two people on the earth who have the same emotions, skillset, knowledge, or personalities. Even though identical twins have so much in common, they are still different people and have different hopes, desires, and personalities.

So, if we are all unique, what will happen if you just adopt someone else's purpose? Will it be accurate? Will it be where you can find real joy and happiness?

What it really comes down to is if you care enough about yourself to diligently search out and find what truly makes you happy and what especially drives you.

As you go throughout this book, you will begin to understand how important it is to honestly understand your own unique purpose and the true understanding, direction, and power it can give you.

What I Found Out

When I went through the process, it took me a while.

I needed to really discover what truly made me happy.

I took a long look at my life through deep meditation and reviewed my past to find when I was the happiest and most excited about life. Personally, my process also involved a significant amount of prayer to understand what God wanted me to do.

The process evolved to much more than just a review of my past through rose-colored glasses. I began to look at my life not just through successes and failures, but instead through the emotions I had while going through all the stages of my life.

When I was finally able to look at my life through "honesty glass," I found that I have had times of tremendous happiness and satisfaction.

These times were all based on helping other people find a measure of happiness.

Over almost 17 years, my wife and I had six children. Our oldest three children came within just over three years, then we had a six and a half year gap before our fourth child arrived, just over four years for our fifth, and just over three more years for our sixth.

So we have had teenagers and little ones in diapers at the same time, which has been a challenge, but has also brought us tremendous blessings.

Fortunately we have been blessed with amazing children who have great hearts and great outlooks on life.

The reason I am sharing this information with you is because it has had a tremendous impact on my life. As my children have grown up, our talks that reach into the wee hours of the morning have increased tremendously.

The conversations changed from trying to understand how to build the best Lego® scene, to how to help them through challenges with friends, and how to make major decisions in life.

Through it all, I was always happiest when I was able to help each of them come to their own resolution and see the light go on in their own mind and figure out for themselves what they should do.

It has been the same thing for me in business. Over the past 20 plus years, I have helped tens of thousands of people learn how to start and grow their businesses.

I have had the opportunity to train people by the thousands and see certain individuals get it and run with it.

When I get the chance to talk with people in small groups or one on one, I can get much more personal, and I have been able to give them direct ideas and watch the light go on in their minds and grasp the realization that they can do it.

As I looked back on all these experiences, I realized that what really makes me tick is when I help other people find the light that helps them make the right choices for happiness within themselves.

So my purpose or "why" is a simple statement, but at the same time it means so much to me and actually guides and directs almost everything I do in my personal and professional life.

Here it is, my purpose or "why":

I thrive when I look at someone smile and know that I contributed to it.

I have also taken the time to really develop an understanding of my purpose or "why." Here is the long version of my purpose or "why":

When I look at someone and see distress in their eyes, I wonder what I can do to help them. I want to help them clarify their thoughts, feelings, or whatever caused their distress.

When I see a prospective or new business owner with the glazed look in their eyes that says: "What am I

doing and how can I make this work?" I really light up as I help them, because I thrive when I'm helping people make sense of it all.

It might even be my wife or one of my children (I have six) who is having a rough day, so I have a lot of opportunities to help people figure out what they need to do to find solutions.

Ultimately, my joy is full when I can make a difference in someone's life. I want to find a way to make things work. I love feeling the joy of seeing a smile in someone that may not have been there before. I love seeing the light go on in someone's mind.

It really is a simple statement and many people probably have a similar feeling, but it is everything to me. I love to see my wife smile. I love to see my children smile. I love helping people and seeing them smile.

Understanding my purpose has given me a great deal of power and influence over my own life. I now can measure whatever I go into, against my own purpose to help me make a good decision and choice about anything I approach.

I hope that sharing my personal experience here helps you understand how powerful knowing your purpose or "why" can really be. It can be the guiding force and affect everything you do.

Chapter 2

Purpose First Decision Making

Understanding your purpose is critical for your happiness, but how does it really help you? How does knowing why you are here on the earth really make a difference in your life? Those are fantastic questions and the answers are found in decision making.

We all have the ability to make choices about everything we do. In the simplest form, every question has at least three very basic answers:

1. Yes
2. No
3. Maybe

For example, if someone asks you if the sky is blue you could say: "Yes it is," "No it's gray," or if you are color blind, you could say, "Maybe."

Understanding the purpose of the question could possibly make a difference on how seriously you consider it and how you respond. If the purpose of the question is to determine if it might rain and you want to protect a newborn baby, your answer would probably be much more thorough.

As the situation becomes more complex and your answer more important, your decision takes on a much deeper meaning.

Here is a little exercise for you to try:

Write down a more than casual decision that you made recently, and then answer the following questions:

1. What went into making the decision?
2. What was the process you used?
3. Was it a conscious or subconscious decision?
4. What influenced your decision?
5. Did you worry about your decision?
6. Did you feel peace about your decision?
7. Did you have confidence in your decision?
8. What were your feelings before and after your decision?
9. What were the consequences, good or bad, about your decision?

After you have examined your decision, do you think you made a purposeful choice? Did you consider how you used your talents, skills, and knowledge to make a decision that aligns with who you are and what you stand for?

If you'd had your purpose defined in a simple statement, would it have helped you make a better decision?

Choices are Not Optional

We make many decisions every day. They can be automatic decisions, such as how to brush your teeth. They can also be very complex decisions, such as "Should I make a career change?" All the decisions you make are not optional, because even if you choose not to decide, you are making a decision not to act.

Power in your life comes when you take charge of yourself and make the decision to act, instead of making the decision to be acted upon.

Acting for yourself is proactive and involves you being present and taking charge of your life.

Being acted upon equates to giving up control of your life to others, letting them make the choices for you. You cannot control how others may act. They may choose to have good motives, or they may act with deceit, malice, selfishness, or in other ways to make their life better at your expense.

Having your purpose defined will enable you to make better choices. When a choice is placed before you, you can immediately evaluate it to see if it is in harmony with your purpose. If it is, you can continue to evaluate it to see if it is worth saying yes to, but if it isn't, the decision becomes simple.

For example, if I were to have a decision of whether or not to have a Buffalo wing birthday party at my house and feed 100 college students, I could evaluate it against my purpose or why: I thrive when I look at someone smile and know that I contributed to it.

My son who just had his 23rd birthday is the person who I replaced the "someone" with in my why statement.

The party would require me having to clean my house to get ready for the party, spending over 12 hours baking 50 pounds of Buffalo wings, making a huge potato salad, and entertaining all the guests for four hours during the party.

For me the decision was easy. I thrive when I see my son smile and seeing him smile was easily worth cooking all day to make him happy.

Yes, we did have between 75 and 100 people here for the party and we could have easily gone through 80 pounds of wings and twice as much potato salad. It was a blast!

By being able to use my purpose to evaluate the decision, it made it a lot easier to be motivated to make the party happen.

What would happen if you went to a job interview and you did not know your purpose? During the interview you might have felt like you would not be a great fit, but the money was good. Could you make the decision to take the job knowing you would be unhappy? Could you make the decision to decline the job because you know you would be unhappy? Could you make any decision at all?

At times, we need to look ahead and make long-term decisions that are based on our purpose. For example, what if you went to the same job interview that we mentioned above and even though the job may not be the right fit for you now, you accept it because it will help you fulfill your purpose in another way.

I was speaking with a friend who was having a hard time applying his purpose to his current business. He was unable to find passion in what he was doing, and he was having a very difficult time with it. As we discussed it, we found that he wants to create a business that is based on importing goods from Peru. Since most goods were made in factories that were sweat shops, he wants to create an ecosystem that pays people real, honest wages for their work in Peru and then import and sell the goods in the United States. But he didn't know how to get enough money to get his idea off the ground.

When we discussed his current business, even though he was not excited or passionate about it, it had great potential for generating a strong cash flow. He could then take some of the profits and put them into the Peruvian import business, which fit his purpose and is what he is passionate about. So he could use his current business to fulfill his long-term goal.

Decisions in and of themselves can be very challenging. However, by having your purpose defined, you have the ability to immediately qualify the decision and determine if it matches your purpose, greatly simplifying the process.

What about Consequences?

Every decision comes with consequences. Sometimes, you may make a decision that is in alignment with your purpose, but could have potentially challenging consequences. For example, you want to work for a nonprofit. Even though the money may not be very good, it fulfills your purpose, so you may choose to accept those consequences.

What happens when you think the consequences of the decision you make will not be severe and you think you can handle them? Well, if a plane is just one degree off course, it could mean ending up missing its destination by hundreds of miles. By having your purpose defined, you have a great tool to help you make the exact decision that would be best for you, keeping your life on course, and helping you avoid severe consequences.

Purpose-filled decisions will always give you a better chance to live a life on your terms than making a decision without purpose.

Chapter 3

How Does Having a Defined Purpose Affect Your Life?

What could happen in your life if you were to have a defined purpose or "why"? Would it make any difference? Would you be happier? Would your life be better?

I think it will be valuable to have you look at different scenarios to help you see the difference of living with a defined purpose as opposed to living without one.

You as an Individual

With Purpose:

Your life is at your command. You make decisions based on a predefined path. You know where you are headed. You accept challenges that are placed in front of you. You have the ability to face difficult decisions and make purposeful choices. When you make a mistake, you accept it and learn from it. You are a person who has confidence and people see it. You are not cocky, egotistical, or haughty. You are humble and driven to live your purpose and find happiness.

Without Purpose:

Your life is a series of events that flow from one place to another. You have no real direction. You are bothered and oftentimes very jealous and disturbed at other people's success and happiness. You willingly or unwillingly sabotage yourself and others when happiness is obtainable. You find excuses to not succeed. You don't have any idea what success is for yourself. No matter how hard you try, it just isn't good enough. You try to please everybody, because you can never please yourself.

You as a College Student

With Purpose:

You enter college with a defined direction. You know what makes you want what you want. Even if you decide to change your major, it is because you have found something that you are even more excited about than when you came into college. You find joy in your out of class activities, hanging out with friends, and club involvement. You are passionate about your studies. You get good grades. You find it helpful to work with others. You find joy in others' success. You are a good roommate. You are genuinely secure with yourself and help others find security in themselves. You are confident about your life after college.

Without Purpose:

You don't get it. You have no idea what you want to do. You spend your time trying to figure out your life. You don't want to spend the money to flip flop on your direction all the time. You change your major hoping that you can find something you like. You hate studying all the time. You are consistently discouraged by your lack of motivation and desire. You look at people and are jealous that they seem to have life figured out. You are constantly questioning your heart and if you even want to be at college.

Your Job or Career

With Purpose:

You wake up and want to go to work. You see problems as opportunities. You work well with others. You are on top of your tasks. You contribute to and support your team. You challenge with intent when you see something that is not right. You are a "company" person who cares about all aspects of your responsibilities. You even care about things outside of your position because you care about the company. You respect others' positions and you want to help others succeed. You go the extra mile to make things better for your coworkers and company.

Without Purpose:

You are burdened by going to work. Your job is just for a paycheck. If it doesn't benefit you, you will not give it your best. You are concerned about yourself and not about the company. You give very little effective work. Your sights are set on the weekend, not on the work. You have anxiety about going to work. You have no desire to help others. If there is a problem, you stay away from it. If you are assigned a task, you do just as much as you have to and nothing more. You really don't care. Your job is a means to an end. Your focus is on things outside of work.

You as a Business Owner

With Purpose:

You know what you are doing. You know when you need to learn and you go get the knowledge. You have a passion for what you do. You support your employees. You care about your product. You care about what people think about your product. You have defined goals outside of finances. You are focused on providing the best for your employees and customers. You care about your customers and how they feel about your product. You make processes for your business to help your employees do things right. You create scenarios for success. You are excited to go to your business and make things happen.

Without Purpose:

You do just what you have to do to make things happen. You may work hard, but you don't go the extra mile to really understand how you can make your business better. You feel that all the time you put in doesn't matter. You are there for the money and nothing else. When it gets hard to make money, you have a hard time giving your all to your business. There is no light at the end of the tunnel and you feel trapped.

Your Marriage

With Purpose:

Your spouse completes you. You find joy in everyday living. You willingly listen. You are interested in how you can help each other. Your compassion is apparent. When your spouse is hurting, you want to help. You argue very infrequently. You desire to make your spouse happy. You do things for your spouse and your marriage because you want to. There are few "have to's" in your marriage. You genuinely want your spouse to be happy. Conversations are two-way events.

Without Purpose:

Happiness is not a regular occurrence in your everyday life with your spouse. You are discouraged in your relationship. You have little in common. You strive to put your needs above your spouse's needs. You are the martyr. You find ways to criticize your spouse. You spend time finding fault. You seldom forgive. Your marriage is a burden.

You as a Teenager

With Purpose:

You are a light to others. You have focus. Your studies are good. You choose good friends. You know why you are in school. You get along with your family. You have good relationships with your siblings. You are kind to your teachers. People search you out to be around you. You have fun. You are drawn to things you are in harmony with. You are a good person. You are kind. You find ways to make others feel good about themselves. Life is good.

Without Purpose:

You don't know where you belong on any given day. You don't care about school, or you only care because your parents say you should. You feel like you don't belong. You don't have friends who encourage you to do good. You feel like you are a burden. You are lonely. You feel like an outcast. You don't get along with teachers or other leaders. You are trying to find your way, but you are constantly frustrated.

Your Family

With Purpose:

You are a team. You work together. You find reasons to appreciate each other. You miss each other when you are not near each other. You have harmony and direction. You understand each other when you talk. You respect each other. You value the opinion of each member of the family. You listen when any member of the family talks, no matter how young or old. You want each family member to be successful. You want to know the hopes and dreams of each family member. You smile when they smile. You cry when they cry. You feel joy when they feel joy. You feel hurt when they hurt. You are a common unit together.

Without Purpose:

You live together, but you don't love together. You are individuals in every sense of the word. You love your family, but you don't like your family. You do not take the time to show them you care. You don't celebrate successes. Your heart is not in the relationships. You're better off disconnecting because you don't care. You care more about your friends than your family. You feel like they don't care, so why should you.

Your Friends

With Purpose:

You have fun together. You are there when they need you. You find reasons to be together. You are comfortable when there is silence. You enjoy doing things together. You can say no without repercussions. You can be yourself. You can help others be themselves. You can share your fears. You can be scared. You can be vulnerable. You can be yourself. You are comfortable being honest. You are happy when you are together.

Without Purpose:

You are at the mercy of others. You are not heard. People take advantage of you. You are uncomfortable with others. You feel pushed into doing things. Your voice is ignored and degraded. If you are not pleasing others, they don't care about you. People only want you for what you can give them. People don't care about you. People ignore you. People use you. People do what they want to you to make themselves happy.

You as a Community Member

With Purpose:

You are united in a common cause where you want to be. You serve happily. You find joy when people reach a common goal. You understand your role and accept it willingly. You believe that you are where you are supposed to be. Your beliefs are in harmony with those around you. You help people perform the best they can. You encourage participation. You feel part of something bigger. You are excited to contribute with your heart and soul. Your contributions are appreciated.

Without Purpose:

You feel like you don't belong. You don't know why you are associating with these people. You feel judged. You are not appreciated. You are not part of something bigger. You are being used and trampled on. The community is a farce. You feel there is no direction. You shouldn't try because no one else is trying. You don't openly commit to the community because it doesn't matter. You don't really know what matters. You don't understand why people are excited. You are alone.

The ability to live with a defined purpose is one of the most valuable parts of our lives and could be the difference between living a life of happiness or misery.

Purpose does matter. Your own individual purpose does matter. Your feelings do matter. But what does it all mean?

The Purpose of Purpose

Chapter 4

What Does it Mean to Live a Purpose First Life?

You now know what a purpose is, how your purpose affects your choices, and how knowing your purpose can affect your life.

But what does it all mean? Is living a purpose first life the magic solution to all of your problems? Is it the thing that will make you happy forever and fix everything wrong in your life? What does knowing your individual purpose really mean to you and only you?

First and foremost, knowing your purpose is not the magic wand that makes all of your problems go away. Nothing will ever do that.

We have something on this planet called agency or free will. We all are free to act for ourselves. We can choose whatever we want. But the catch is that our choices come with consequences that we cannot control.

If you choose to go 100 miles per hour on a small dirt road, you must be ready to accept the consequences of either having a blast or skidding and sliding off the road, rolling the car 10 times, and being killed in the process.

If you choose to eat a poisonous blowfish, you have to accept either having some of the best tasting fish anywhere, or the risk of the chef cooking it improperly and you die.

If you choose to skydive, you have to accept the consequences of either having your parachute open and living, or staying closed and dying.

Other choices are out of your control, such as having another car come down the road at 100 miles per hour, having it hit you when it rolls over, and it kills you.

Since we all have agency, and we all make many choices every day, our choices will affect how we live our lives and how others live theirs.

Have you ever thought about the different kinds of lives you might live? Have you ever wondered what the consequences are of living a different kind of life? Let's look at a few of the different kinds of life you can lead and hopefully we can understand more about it.

Living a Purpose First Life

- What it is: Living a life where decisions are made based on a defined purpose.
- Consequences: You live a life of passion. You find things that resonate with you and they make you

happy. You are attached to a cause. You are always looking at making things happen to bring about your purpose. You say no to things that do not match your purpose, thereby freeing yourself from burdensome activities.

Living a Me First Life

- What it is: Living a life where decisions are made based on you and only you, regardless of how anyone else is affected.

- Consequences: You are alone. You are only concerned about yourself, so no one is ever really concerned about you. You don't find joy in others, so you are only happy when you succeed. You feel intense jealousy, since only you matter. It is hard for you to let anyone inside your personal space, unless you want to use them for something. It's always "What about me?" not "I'm happy for you."

Living a Money First Life

- What it is: Living your life where decisions are based on money and nothing else matters.

- Consequences: People don't matter. Only money matters. You hurt other people and it doesn't really matter to you. As long as you get paid, it doesn't matter what rules or "guidelines" you follow or break. You don't care about the feelings of others. Your family comes second to or lower than money. You work hard for your family, but in reality it is for you to gain money and power. You keep score and you are only happy if you win. Period.

It's kind of obvious what kind of life would bring the most joy, isn't it?

When you live a purpose first life, you make choices that will bring about the best outcome possible. You will be directed to live in a way that brings joy to yourself and others and not intentionally harm others. You will find reasons to celebrate happiness and shun destructive behaviors. You will build others up and help them find joy.

In short, you have a reason to live a good life, and you know the direction you need to go to live it.

So the next question is the all-important question: How do I find my purpose? Read on, and I will show you a method that can do just that.

Chapter 5

Finding Your Purpose

What do you need to do to create your own defined purpose?

Is it hard? Maybe a little.

Is it worth it? Yes.

Is the time to do it right now? Definitely.

I have discovered a way to help you discover what it is deep within yourself that makes you tick. It is something that once you have completed the process, you will say to yourself: "Of course that is my purpose."

You will find that when you are going through this process, you will either be stumped, or not be able to write fast enough. You will either be drawn into deep introspection, or not be able to stop laughing.

These are all parts of you that need to come out.

First let me make something crystal clear. This is something that is definitive and without exception for every human being on earth:

Your purpose on this earth is what makes you happy deeply inside your soul.

There are probably over seven billion ways that this happiness can be identified because there are over seven billion people on the earth, but it is still true that what makes you truly happy is your real purpose.

Why? Because isn't that the whole point of our life on this earth, to bring true happiness and joy to ourselves and others? What else can you reach inside and find that defines you?

Are we all at our best when we find happiness?

If you choose to disagree with me, that is according to your agency and free will. But I want to give you a distinct challenge to complete this exercise and see what the results are. I know you will find that you have a specific purpose in life and it is related to what brings you true happiness and joy.

Some of you will say "I don't need to do this exercise because I already know my purpose." I believe that you can know your purpose in your heart and live by it. But let me ask you this question, would it help you to be able to find a clear and concise statement about your purpose? If so, I hope that you will complete this exercise, because it can change your life just as it has changed the lives of many others to have a simply defined purpose.

When you complete this exercise and have a clear and concise statement of what your purpose in life is, you can use it in every aspect of your life. Believe me when I say that it can be a complete life-changing experience, even a very emotional experience, to identify and feel in your heart why you are personally here on this planet and what you are meant to do for yourself and the rest of humanity.

The Purpose Finding Process

1. Write it Down

Take a look back at your life and identify experiences where you know you were happy, excited, motivated, desirous, or where you were yearning for something to happen. Your list should include upwards of 300 different experiences.

This is the most important step in the entire process. Take your time. You may want to complete it in a few hours or spread it out over a few days or weeks. You may find that once you get started, you won't be able to stop. You may also want to speak with people who know you well to have them bring experiences to your mind that you may not remember yourself.

Here is a little memory jogger for you to help bring things back to your memory:

1. What is your earliest happy memory?

2. What do you remember about being around a favorite aunt or uncle?

3. What do you remember about playing games with your parents and siblings?

4. How did you feel when your friend gave you a hug?

5. Did you have fun dancing?

6. What happened when you were five years old?

7. What happy experiences happened each year of your life (age 6, age 7, and so on)?

8. How did you feel when you met your spouse?

9. How did you feel when you had your very first kiss?

10. How did it feel when you were driving your car?

11. What toys did you like playing with when you were a child?

12. Do you remember how you felt when you got your first job?

13. How did you feel when you graduated from high school or college?

14. What do you remember about the first time you put your feet in a lake or in the ocean?

15. How did you feel when you saw a beautiful sunset?

16. Do you remember riding a bike and having fun all day long?

17. What do you remember about playing baseball, soccer, football, basketball, or even badminton?

18. How did it feel when you made a basket or hit a home run?

19. Do you remember going out to dinner on a special day?

20. What was it like when you finished making a special dinner?

This is just a short list to help you remember happy times.

Now you need to start writing. I have places for you to write down 300 memories, so please take advantage of it and make it work for you. You may not need all 300 spots, but I want you to realize the power of having a lot of memories written down when you go through the other steps of the process. Please write down at least 100, but try for as many as possible.

1. _____
2. _____
3. _____
4. _____
5. _____
6. _____
7. _____
8. _____
9. _____
10. _____

11. _____

12. _____

13. _____

14. _____

15. _____

16. _____

17. _____

18. _____

19. _____

20. _____

21. _____

22. _____

23. _____

24. _____

25. _____

26. _____

27. _____

28. _____

29. _____

30. _____

31. _____

32. _____

33. _____

34. _____
35. _____
36. _____
37. _____
38. _____
39. _____
40. _____
41. _____
42. _____
43. _____
44. _____
45. _____
46. _____
47. _____
48. _____
49. _____
50. _____
51. _____
52. _____
53. _____
54. _____
55. _____
56. _____

57. _____

58. _____

59. _____

60. _____

61. _____

62. _____

63. _____

64. _____

65. _____

66. _____

67. _____

68. _____

69. _____

70. _____

71. _____

72. _____

73. _____

74. _____

75. _____

76. _____

77. _____

78. _____

79. _____

Finding Your Purpose

80. _____
81. _____
82. _____
83. _____
84. _____
85. _____
86. _____
87. _____
88. _____
89. _____
90. _____
91. _____
92. _____
93. _____
94. _____
95. _____
96. _____
97. _____
98. _____
99. _____
100. _____
101. _____
102. _____

103. _____

104. _____

105. _____

106. _____

107. _____

108. _____

109. _____

110. _____

111. _____

112. _____

113. _____

114. _____

115. _____

116. _____

117. _____

118. _____

119. _____

120. _____

121. _____

122. _____

123. _____

124. _____

125. _____

126. _____
127. _____
128. _____
129. _____
130. _____
131. _____
132. _____
133. _____
134. _____
135. _____
136. _____
137. _____
138. _____
139. _____
140. _____
141. _____
142. _____
143. _____
144. _____
145. _____
146. _____
147. _____
148. _____

149. _____
150. _____
151. _____
152. _____
153. _____
154. _____
155. _____
156. _____
157. _____
158. _____
159. _____
160. _____
161. _____
162. _____
163. _____
164. _____
165. _____
166. _____
167. _____
168. _____
169. _____
170. _____
171. _____

172. _____
173. _____
174. _____
175. _____
176. _____
177. _____
178. _____
179. _____
180. _____
181. _____
182. _____
183. _____
184. _____
185. _____
186. _____
187. _____
188. _____
189. _____
190. _____
191. _____
192. _____
193. _____
194. _____

195. _____

196. _____

197. _____

198. _____

199. _____

200. _____

201. _____

202. _____

203. _____

204. _____

205. _____

206. _____

207. _____

208. _____

209. _____

210. _____

211. _____

212. _____

213. _____

214. _____

215. _____

216. _____

217. _____

218. _____
219. _____
220. _____
221. _____
222. _____
223. _____
224. _____
225. _____
226. _____
227. _____
228. _____
229. _____
230. _____
231. _____
232. _____
233. _____
234. _____
235. _____
236. _____
237. _____
238. _____
239. _____
240. _____

241. _____
242. _____
243. _____
244. _____
245. _____
246. _____
247. _____
248. _____
249. _____
250. _____
251. _____
252. _____
253. _____
254. _____
255. _____
256. _____
257. _____
258. _____
259. _____
260. _____
261. _____
262. _____
263. _____

264. _____

265. _____

266. _____

267. _____

268. _____

269. _____

270. _____

271. _____

272. _____

273. _____

274. _____

275. _____

276. _____

277. _____

278. _____

279. _____

280. _____

281. _____

282. _____

283. _____

284. _____

285. _____

286. _____

The Purpose of Purpose

287. _____

288. _____

289. _____

290. _____

291. _____

292. _____

293. _____

294. _____

295. _____

296. _____

297. _____

298. _____

299. _____

300. _____

2. Identify Key Elements

As you read your list, start to identify key words, themes, common words, feelings, desires, or other key indicators that show up again and again. This is another reason to have as many memories as possible in the list above. I have provided 25 spots below, but it may be more or less than this. The important thing is to really dig into the memories that you have written down and carefully analyze them to find the important elements.

1. _____
2. _____
3. _____
4. _____
5. _____
6. _____
7. _____
8. _____
9. _____
10. _____
11. _____
12. _____
13. _____
14. _____
15. _____

16. _____
17. _____
18. _____
19. _____
20. _____
21. _____
22. _____
23. _____
24. _____
25. _____

3. Finding the Overall Message

When you look at your key elements, do you see an overall message? If not, look closer, because it is there. If you are religious, you may want to make this a matter of communication with God or your higher power.

_____
_____
_____
_____
_____

4. Verify Your Purpose

Be careful about this next step, because even though it is very powerful, you want to be careful who you choose to help you.

Share your experience with someone who will support you in your quest for learning your purpose. Make sure that you are willing to receive a few compliments and some criticism.

If you are not ready for the criticism, you can skip this step, but realize that you will not be receiving feedback and having someone push you to make it better. You can also just suck it up, and fight for your beliefs. When someone pushes back at you, you need to realize that it will make your defined purpose statement even stronger.

_____

_____

_____

_____

_____

5. Make Adjustments

Make any final adjustments to the wording. Your final wording is very important, as it will guide you for many years to come. You will also depend upon the wording to help you evaluate opportunities from all aspects of your life.

_____

_____

_____

_____

6. What is Your Defined Purpose or "Why"?

_____

_____

_____

_____

_____

I have shared my purpose or "why" with you earlier, "I thrive when I look at someone smile and know that I contributed to it." I believe it with my whole heart and soul and it is very personal to me.

Just by putting it out there, I realize that some people may choose not to respect it the way I do. But I know that it is important for you to have an example, so you can go out and discover your own "why." After all, that is what would make me happy, knowing that you have a smile in your heart because you know your purpose (your "why"). That is what drives me.

Now that you know your purpose or "why," you should evaluate all that you do against it.

For example, you could use your purpose or "why" to evaluate a business opportunity. Is the opportunity in harmony with your "why"? If you look back at yourself in a few years, will you say "I am glad I did it"?

If the opportunity is in harmony with your purpose, you will be able to push through any challenges and withstand any resistance placed against you. You may or may not succeed, but you will know that you have lived with purpose in mind for your life.

If the opportunity is not in harmony with your purpose, stop now. Don't waste your time trying to make something work that you are not committed to. You will not only fail in that particular opportunity, but the repercussions in your life may be severe.

Next, we will examine how to ask purpose first questions to help you make full use of your defined purpose statement.

The Purpose of Purpose

Chapter 6

Purpose First Questions

What is a purpose first question? It is a question that combines your purpose with a question. It may seem awkward to think you need to involve your purpose in every question you ask and every decision you make, but think this through with me for a few moments.

Have you ever thought about the process we go through when we ask a question and make a decision? The following is a simple breakdown of the process.

1. **You have an idea come to your mind.**

    It could be a question like one of the following:

    • Should I turn right at the stop sign?

    • Should I eat a burger or a chicken sandwich?

    • Should I look for a new job?

    • Should I brush my teeth this morning?

2. **You consider the idea.**

   You think about the question and determine the options you have.

3. **You evaluate your options.**

   You use your experience, knowledge, and feelings to measure each option and determine how beneficial it would be to choose a particular option.

4. **You decide on the best option to answer the question and proceed.**

When you answer the question at hand, you make a judgment call about what is the best answer for you to choose. A simple question like brushing your teeth could become complicated if you are going to have dental work done and you have significant pain in your mouth. You may want to postpone brushing your teeth until after the procedure.

In reality, we answer hundreds if not thousands of questions we ask ourselves every day. Most questions we answer are automatic and simple, but there are many every day that require us to break out our experiences and knowledge, and think before we make a decision.

What if you were able to add your defined purpose into making decisions for every question you have? What kind of life would you be able to lead if your personal purpose was involved in every question? How would it change what you do?

Let's take the above example of what kind of sandwich you are going to eat and enhance it with your defined purpose.

1. **You have an idea come to your mind.**

   You want to know what you should eat for lunch.

2. **You consider the idea.**

   You discover two options for today: a hamburger or a chicken sandwich.

3. **You evaluate your options.**

   In this case, your basic evaluation includes taste, desire, and possibly many other factors. But if you add in your defined purpose, it could change. For example, using my purpose of "I thrive when I look at someone smile and know that I contributed to it" could influence me in several ways.

   - If I am the someone who I want to see smile, and I love hamburgers, my choice would be a hamburger.

   - If my wife is the someone who I want to see smile, I may choose the healthier chicken sandwich option.

   - If I am with a friend who is the someone, I may want to eat in harmony with what they are having to share in the experience.

   By adding in the defined purpose, I add an entire different criteria for my decision. One that is based on my purpose.

4. **You determine the best option.**

In the end, I chose to make myself smile and eat the tasty hamburger.

In reality, the question took only seconds to make and involving my defined purpose influenced the decision heavily without taking virtually any extra time.

What if you could train yourself to make decisions based on your defined purpose in everything you do? It may seem like a lot of work, but in reality it is just a little training for your mind that inserts your defined purpose into each question you ask.

For example, if I have the following question on my mind, how would my defined purpose statement help?

"Should I go to work today, even though I feel sick?"

Without my defined purpose, I could simply call it a day before it even starts, and stay home.

With my defined purpose, I realize that I am not really that sick and I have an important project to work on that is time sensitive and important to get done. Since I thrive when I see someone smile, if I go to work and finish the project, everyone involved will be happy, and I fulfill my purpose.

It's a simple example, but when you involve your purpose in your decisions, you are living a life that will bring you meaning, happiness, and fulfillment.

The question you should ask is: "What option(s) are in harmony with my purpose?"

When you insert that question into your everyday life for every question you ask, your decisions end up being based on your purpose.

When you make purposeful decisions, your life will change at the very root of your being.

When your life is directed by your purpose, you become happier, better to be around, and are driven by a passion that is contagious to those around you.

When you are dealing with a significant issue, and you involve your purpose in your questioning and decision making, you have a powerful influence to help you stay true to yourself.

The Purpose of Purpose

Chapter 7

Finding Passion through Purpose

If purpose is "why something is done," passion is the "consuming desire to do it."

We have all met passionate people who we marvel at. They are the people who just won't stop and are never ending in their desire to make something happen.

We all have the opportunity to have passion about something. In fact, I believe that even when we are at our lowest point, we can still find passion in our lives.

What comes first, passion or purpose? Well, it is hard to have passion about something you don't believe in. Therefore, purpose must come first.

I have shown you a way to find your purpose, which is what makes you truly happy in life, and that is the foundation for finding passion. You can't be passionate about something that does not bring you joy.

Think about it for a minute.

What is something that you know you are passionate about? One of my passions is driving a convertible. I have had more than one in my life and I love everything about it. I love getting in the car and opening the top. I love the feeling of the sun hitting me as the top goes down. I love the feeling of putting on my sunglasses and looking up into the sky. I love the wind rushing through my hair. I love listening to the rumble of the engine as I get up to speed. I love driving on a warm summer night and seeing the stars in the sky. I love having my wife next to me enjoying everything with me. I love it when my kids are so excited to ride with me. I love going fast and experiencing life with the top down. It feels like there are no borders, and I can be in touch with everything on heaven and earth.

To understand how this example fits into discovering passion, let's look at the formula.

First, remember my purpose: "I thrive when I look at someone smile and know that I contributed to it."

Second, I had a big idea. That idea was driving a convertible. I had always wanted to since I was a kid, and I was always in awe of convertible sports cars.

Third, I determined that the big idea of getting a convertible was in harmony with my purpose in life, which was helping people smile. In this case, the someone that I was excited to see smile was myself. This is not being a self-centered person, or even being a person first instead of purpose first individual. Instead, it is being true to oneself and making sure that we take care of ourselves in our everyday lives. If your purpose involves helping others in any way, make sure you remember who you look at in the mirror every morning. You must continually help yourself to make sure you are in a position to be able to help others.

I took action. When the opportunity came to get a convertible, I jumped at the chance. I was so excited to drive the car with the top down. I had loud music playing and the wind in my hair was amazing. I was able to smile for myself and for those around me. When I give people a ride in my car, I see their faces light up and their grins get big. Almost everyone who rides with me finds a great deal of joy having the wind in their hair and the ability to see the world in a 360 degree way.

We can simplify the process into a basic formula that makes it easy to understand.

Purpose + Big Idea that is in Harmony with Purpose = Passion

When you discover an idea that is in harmony with your purpose, you can create a passion for it.

When you meet someone who is in harmony with your purpose, you can work together with a passion for your common purpose.

When you find a job that is in harmony with your purpose, you can feel passion for it.

When you find a cause that is in harmony with your purpose, you can get behind it with passion.

The real question you should be asking yourself now is: "What do I feel passionate about in life and what does not move me at all?"

Chapter 8

How to Let Your Purpose Direct Your Life

What is the key to having purpose direct your life?

Is it placing your defined purpose on sticky notes everywhere in your life? Is it stressing out to make sure that you have your purpose memorized and making sure that everything is exact and detailed about how your purpose is directing you?

Of course not!

It's about having your purpose direct you from inside your soul. Remember that you have defined the purpose that you already had within you. You didn't create it from scratch. In fact, the exercise of how you wrote down hundreds of memories that made you happy only brought to your mind what you have already experienced in life.

Your defined purpose is not new to you, it is just easier to identify and remember. Now, when you go throughout life, you have something to gauge how you are living your life every day.

So what can you do on a daily basis that will help you remember your purpose, use your purpose to help you, and gain a better life day by day?

Simply ask yourself four questions every day.

What time during the day you ask the questions is up to you, but if you are consistent, you will find tremendous results.

Each one of these questions needs to be framed within your purpose:

Question 1: **What am I doing right?**

Question 2: **What is keeping me from improving?**

Question 3: **How do I define success for the next time period?**

Question 4: **What are five happy memories from the past (hour, day, week, or life)?**

How are these four questions going to make a dramatic difference in your life? What significance do they hold? Let's look at each question in depth to discover how it will help you let your purpose direct your life.

Question 1: **What am I doing right?**

What are you doing right in regard to your purpose? As you go throughout the day making decisions, interacting with your family, thinking about yourself, thinking about others, doing your job, running your business, learning, teaching, and any other activity, how are you doing? What are the things you are doing right? Are you living by your purpose or are you being acted upon and letting life take you where it wants? Remember that inaction is a choice and it allows you to be controlled by others. Are you standing up for your beliefs?

You can write down one thing you are doing right, or many things. Just write down what you can handle.

Question 2:   What is keeping me from improving?

Do not beat yourself up. Instead, use this question to identify something that you can change to better yourself. Do not list more than one item a day. Your goal is to live by your purpose, not to tear yourself down because you make mistakes. Everyone on the planet makes mistakes, but those who can identify them, address them, and work on them are the ones who make significant growth in their lives.

Question 3:   How do I define success for the next time period?

What is success to you? When you have a definition for success for a time period, you can be fulfilled. You need to understand what success means to you. Your defined purpose is a great standard and a tremendous place to go for inspiration.

For example, when I use my purpose as my standard for success, my life stays on track. I do all I can to bring joy to others. So my definition of success could be making a meeting a good experience for everyone there or treating my children with respect and love.

You can choose to be successful at all times. Defining success before you enter into a situation will help you make the right choices for the right reasons.

Question 4:   What are five happy memories from the past (hour, day, week, or life)?

Why include this in your daily questions? You have already defined your purpose and written out hundreds of memories. Do you still need to continue to do it?

Yes. But why?

You do not live your life by one experience, instead you create new experiences every day. What happens when you bring five new happy memories to light every day? You become happier. It really is that simple.

By identifying how your happy memories of today relate to other times in your life, you are able to help bring a longer-term feeling of happiness for your entire life.

Results

By being dedicated to living by your purpose, you will find out how much better life can be.

I have seen people overcome addiction, depression, and other challenges by simply changing their outlook. (It works for some, but not all.) Can you imagine what you can create in your life by simply living by your purpose?

Chapter 9

Purpose First Leadership

What about leadership? It may seem that leading by purpose is a great idea, and it is. But how do you do it and what difference does it really make?

At its most basic, leadership is leading a group of people or an organization.

But when you start carefully considering and understanding leadership, you begin to see how a person becomes a leader.

A number of years ago, I attended a lecture given by Stephen R. Covey, author of "The 7 Habits of Highly Effective People," one of the bestselling books of all time. He gave perhaps the most complete and powerful definition of leadership I have ever heard.

"Leadership is communicating a person's worth and potential so clearly, that they are inspired to see it in themselves."
~ Stephen R. Covey

Who can do that? What does it take to communicate a person's worth and potential? How does knowing your own purpose fit into this equation?

Let's break it down.

When you have a defined purpose, you know what you are about personally, you have confidence in yourself, and above all you believe in yourself.

When you are secure in your own purpose, you can communicate and focus on others and truly show an understanding which fosters mutual respect. When you have a mutual respect for each other, you genuinely show you care. When you genuinely care about someone, they feel validated, understood, and valuable. This establishes trust and worth and you are now on common ground. Once on common ground, you can lead people to do great things.

So the real purpose of leadership is to communicate a person's worth and potential clearly, so people can identify with their own worth and potential.

Great! You now know the basics of purpose first leadership, but why does that really matter? How does it help to lead others?

When you compare purpose first leadership with other leadership styles, some significant differences are readily seen. I am taking some liberty to explain a few of these styles in my own way, but you can find extensive definitions in other places. You may also find in these definitions that some of the styles are very loosely called leadership.

Authoritarian leadership is all about complete control by a person. The person in charge knows it all and expects everyone to follow their instructions without exception.

Committee leadership is also about control, but instead of one individual, it is done by committee. Everyone must follow the dictates of the committee, and there is no room for discussion.

Suck up or brown-nosing leadership is when someone is more concerned about impressing someone than by helping the people they are responsible for.

Lazy leadership is getting the credit for the work done by other people.

Angry leadership is when no one is happy about anything because the "leader" just yells at everyone all the time.

Clueless leadership is when the "leader" has no idea what they are doing and doesn't know how to change it.

Depressed leadership is when the "leader" doesn't believe that they can accomplish anything and they don't believe anything or anyone can help them.

Egocentric leadership is when the "leader" is consumed by pride and ego and is never wrong, making life almost unbearable for everyone involved.

Money driven leadership is when the "leader" is focused on money at the expense of everything else. If it doesn't fit in the budget, it doesn't fit. Period.

Perfection leadership is when the leader is focused on perfection, even if it paralyzes everything else.

Tyrant leadership is when the leader is right all the time and they will "kill" you if you don't do exactly what they say.

We could go on and on about the different styles of leadership, but I think you get the idea.

When you compare purpose first leadership with any of these other kinds of "leadership," you can understand why we have a crisis in our world. Very few people practice purpose first leadership and it shows in how people feel they are treated at work, at home, at church, at play, in their communities, and in most any circumstance they encounter.

The importance of living a purpose first life is now even more apparent and more important than ever before. We need a wholesale change in what we do and how we do it all over the world to help us live purpose first. Purpose first leadership is a major part of the answer.

Chapter 10

Purpose First and Achieving Goals

The next component we need to have in order to start creating purpose first families, businesses, communities, or any other type of organization is to understand how critical a purpose is to obtaining whatever outcome you desire.

Typically, when someone wants a specific outcome, which most people simply call a goal, they write down a statement on a piece of paper and more often than not forget about it. Think about how often New Year's resolutions go unfulfilled or how many times you have set a new target weight and missed it. What about when you have set a sales goal for your business and then never look at it again, or when a community organization sets a goal and then focus shifts to a new item and it is forgotten about.

What do we need to do to create goals that mean something so we will work harder to achieve them? We need to change how we look at things. We need to bring purpose into achieving the outcomes we want. We need a strategy that can be applied to everything we do and in every situation we are in. We need to make the outcome we want happen with purpose and a specific plan, not just a note on a napkin we look at a few times and then throw away.

For over 25 years, I have studied and found four common components in almost all the different life and business strategies.

Every strategy focuses on a desired outcome or result.

Every strategy has a reason or a purpose behind it.

Every strategy is almost always accompanied by specific tactics to make the strategy happen.

As the strategy is implemented, it is always evaluated to make sure the tactics are being carried out properly and the desired outcome will be accomplished.

To make it even more simple to remember, I simply call it the "Strategic Action System."

"Strategic Action System"

1. Outcome

Your action strategy should begin with what outcome you desire. You must know what you want to accomplish and be able to visualize it to achieve success.

2. Purpose or "Why"

You need to have the purpose of the outcome you desire clearly identified.

3. How

Every action needs a plan to make it happen. This is also called tactics.

4. Evaluate

Evaluate the entire strategy, constantly looking for ways to improve your plan and make sure you stay on target to get your desired outcome.

When to Use the "Strategic Action System"

The key to success with the "Strategic Action System" is how dedicated you are to using it. Whether you are using it in your personal life, your family, your professional life, your community, or any other aspect of your life, when you use it, you will see great results.

When you first start using it, you should use it all the time. You could set one up for writing an email, making a social media post, making a phone call, driving to pick up children, a project at work, an entire business, your community organization, or anywhere else you can think of.

Several things will happen as you start to use it.

First, you will notice that it takes a lot more time than not using it. That is to be expected since you are trying something new.

Second, you will wonder why you need to use it on simple things like writing an email or a social media post.

Third, once you do it five or ten times, you will understand the power it holds in creating a purpose first mentality for yourself. As you continue to use it, it will become second nature, and you will begin to not have to write everything down all the time. You will find yourself thinking about a desired outcome in your mind, immediately thinking of the purpose for that desired outcome, and then taking planned action to make it happen.

So how does it work? How difficult is it do? Here is an example of how a system may look for a business:

My "Strategic Action System" for My Business

1. Outcome

I want to create a business that will provide long-term financial freedom for my family while being focused on impacting lives.

2. Purpose or Why

I believe in helping others and in turn helping myself.

3. How

I will run a hybrid of an internet business and a drop ship business and sell products on eBay. I will market using social media and also by creating an email marketing system.

4. Evaluate

I will have data on which marketing systems drive sales and learn to adapt and adjust my systems to make them work effectively.

As I run my business, I may need to create additional "Strategic Action Systems" for specific components of my business, including social media marketing, eBay selling, drop ship organization, and many other items.

Understanding what your desired outcome is, why you want it, and how you are going to go about getting it done are very simple yet powerful tools to make your business and even your everyday life successful.

One more thing...

The "Strategic Action System" in and of itself is life changing, but what if there were one more thing that would make it even more powerful? What if you could do something every day that took five minutes and would make you more effective as a person, spouse, parent, friend, worker, community member, or anywhere else in your life?

The following is a true story from almost a century ago which shows the importance of knowing what you need to do and how to go about making it happen. As you read it, picture using the "Strategic Action System" for each item on your list. Also, picture doing this task for every aspect of your life, not just for business.

The Ivy Lee Method

Back in 1918, an efficiency expert named Ivy Lee met with his prospective client, Charles M. Schwab, who was president of Bethlehem Steel. He outlined how his organization could benefit the company. Lee ended his presentation by saying: "With our service, you'll know how to manage better."

Schwab then stated: "We don't need more 'knowing,' but we need more 'doing.' If you can give us something to help us do the things we already know we ought to do, I'll gladly pay you anything within reason you ask."

Lee answered: "I can give you something in twenty minutes that will step up your doing at least fifty percent."

"Okay," Schwab said, "show me."

Lee then handed Schwab a blank sheet of paper and said: "Write down the six most important tasks (no more and no less) you have to do tomorrow in order of their importance. The first thing tomorrow morning, look at item one and start working on it until it is finished.

"Then tackle item two in the same way, and so on. Do this until quitting time. Don't be concerned if you have only finished one or two. Take care of emergencies, but then get back to working on the most important items. The others can wait. At the end of the day, move any unfinished items to a new list of six tasks for the following day.

"Make this a habit every working day. Pass it on to those under you. Try it as long as you like, and then send me your check for what you think it's worth."

In a few weeks, Schwab sent Lee a check for $25,000 (around $400,000 in 2015 dollars) with a letter stating that he learned a profitable lesson.

After five years, this plan was largely responsible for turning the unknown Bethlehem Steel Company into one of the biggest independent steel producers. Schwab purportedly made a hundred million dollars and became one of the best known steel men in the world.*

* The author of this story is unknown, and it has appeared in many different publications with minor variations of how it has been told.

The Purpose of Purpose

Chapter 11

Creating Purpose First Families

The power of having a purpose first family cannot be underestimated.

When you think of what you want your family to be like, here are some of the qualities that may come to mind:

- Strong relationship between husband and wife.
- Each spouse doing all they can to help each other find joy.
- Ability to communicate feelings to your children.
- Have the kind of relationship where you can overcome just about any challenge by working together.
- Ability for your children to express themselves openly without feeling threatened.
- Have a home where you can feel the harmony among all who live there.
- To be able to really talk around the dinner table.

- Have each family member interested in each of the other family member's challenges, successes, interests, desires, goals, opinions, and other things that make them an individual.
- Have everyone celebrate individuality and at the same time have solid unity as a family unit.

These thoughts may seem like a pipe dream to many people. How can you get a family to really do at least one of these items?

Let me share an experience with you about my family. When my wife and I had been married 11 years, we decided to create a statement that established what we stood for that we could hold on to through the thick and thin of family life.

We sat down in our backyard with the three children we had at the time on a gorgeous afternoon and worked through our feelings and beliefs to get to the meat of what we wanted to stand for. We are a religious family, so our traditions reflect our beliefs. The result has stood with us for the past 14 years, and every member of our family has bought into and believes in our statement.

Here it is:

"Each member of our family, will use our heart, might, mind, and strength to stay true and faithful to the principles of the gospel of Jesus Christ. Our goal is to be a family forever."

A few years later, we added a few words to enhance it.

"The McKenzie Family: kindable, strong, courageous, happy, loving, righteous, and willing to work."

One of our little children said the word kindable and we all liked it so much, we kept it (even though it is not actually a word).

Now when we get together for an activity, a family council (family meeting), or sometimes just on a whim, we will give the full statement.

In reality, we have defined our family's purpose and we support each other every step of the way. Don't get me wrong, with six children we have our fair share of arguments, challenges, problems, and heated discussions that have a very emotional element to them. But we also have a unity where we all love to be together. Three of my children are now living away from home, but they support each other and are good friends as well as being siblings.

We also have a tradition. Every night we have a cheer we do as a family. Everyone who is home at the time will join together for an evening prayer, a family hug, and then a cheer where we say: "One, two, three, I love my family, love first!" At least once a day, we tell each member of our family that we love them.

You may have a different experience. You may or may not be religious, have two parents in your home, or have children in your home. The important thing is to find a purpose for your family.

Finding Your Family's Purpose

You can actually use the same process for your family that you used to find your own purpose. When you are listing all the happy memories, have everyone provide input. With everyone participating, you create ownership for each individual for the statement you create. You can list hundreds of happy memories as a family.

You can also define your purpose as a couple. You can list all of the happy memories you have had together throughout your relationship.

You can also help each of your children discover their purpose by following the same pattern.

Using Your Family Purpose

Once you have defined your family's purpose, you can use it in every aspect of your life. You can use it to help you in making decisions, from small ones to major ones. You will have the ability to talk to your children on common ground.

Can you picture the difference between a purpose driven family and one that is not lead by purpose?

Here is an example of a parent – child relationship.

- **A relationship led by a <u>person first</u> model (non-purpose example):**

  When a parent is dedicated to their own self, the children are not put in a position of respect or value. Parents will often work long hours saying it is for the children, when in reality it is for their own ego or gratification. They get frustrated with their children because they have no initiative to accomplish anything the parents tell them to do. The children don't like spending time with their family and often openly rebel because they can tell that the parents are more involved in their own lives than in the lives of their children. When people see that you don't care, they follow your example.

- **A relationship led by a <u>purpose first</u> model:**

  The parents lead by showing full attention to their children. This does not mean that they give into everything the children want, but instead show that they care about what their children say and feel. They put the needs of their family above their own needs, and it shows. Children pick up on this and mutual respect is formed. Children accept that the parents are in the leadership role because they feel validated, heard, their worth is established, and they believe their parents when they are praised and encouraged.

Can you see the difference? Can you see the harmony versus the disconnection of all involved? This is not an easy shift for an existing family, but by working on developing a family purpose together, it can be done.

Then when you have an opportunity to hold a family council, you have a common ground where people know they can be heard and understood. It creates a safe and loving environment when you need to discuss family problems.

Helping your family live a purpose first life will take a little time and effort, but the rewards are tremendous and your family will have a foundation to take you through times of challenge and success.

Chapter 12

Creating Purpose First
Careers and Businesses

As I have consulted with people, I have found people who have little or no direction and others who are passionate about what they do. It doesn't seem to matter if they are working at a job or are the business owner themselves, people who have purpose in what they do are happier.

How does it all work? What difference does it make if you are happy at your job? Why put in the effort to make your job or business a place of happiness? What is it worth to you? Does it matter to you if you live your life in happiness everywhere you go?

Careers

Let's start off by putting questions in the context of the employee, or people who work for someone else. Here is a list of questions that you may ask yourself about your current position:

- Why do you do it?
- Do you know why you chose your current position?
- Do you know if your job is something that you really want to do?
- How do you get along with your coworkers?
- How do you like your boss?
- How do you like the people you supervise?
- How do you feel about the organization of the company?
- Is the company well run?
- Does the business owner take care of their employees?
- Do you like the projects that you work on?
- Do you like doing things for other people in your organization?
- How do you feel when you get up in the morning to go to work?
- How do you feel when you get home from work?
- Do you smile when you are at work?

- Does your job make you crazy?

This list of questions can be directly influenced by your defined purpose. When you know your purpose, you can evaluate each question with confidence and accuracy. This list is by no means comprehensive, but it is a good start in determining if your job fits your purpose.

If it does, more power to you. You are probably finding joy going to work every day and your job has meaning to you.

If your job doesn't fit your purpose, you need help. You need to determine if you can find a way to look at your job to be in harmony with your purpose. You may need to look at your position in a different light to see if you can make it serve your defined purpose. You may also need to start looking for a new position that aligns with your purpose in life either within your company or at a new one. You are the one who needs to make that decision.

There is another idea you can implement at your current position. You can come up with a "big idea" for your job. Your "big idea" could be anything, but make sure it is in harmony with your defined purpose. You may be able to alter how you work, the project that you work on, or anything about your job to make it more in harmony with your purpose. Then, even though there are things you don't like about your job, you have something you can hold on to and create a good environment for yourself and others. You could even encourage your coworkers to discover their purpose and create a support group for each other. If you want to keep your current job, get creative and make it happen.

When you cross your "big idea" with your purpose, you will create passion, which can help carry you through just about anything.

Businesses

Being an employee means that the buck ultimately stops with someone else. But when you own your own business, the buck always stops with you.

- As a business owner, how are you handling that?
- What are you doing to make your business a great place for employees and customers?
- Does your business mean anything to you or is it just a money machine?
- Did you know that when your employees are truly happy, you will be happy too?
- Why run a business based on a purpose?
- Can you even discover a purpose for your business?
- I understand that restaurants operate to feed people, but that is not what I am asking. Instead, can you define a purpose for your business that people can rally around and find meaning in?

How I have helped people find the purpose for their business is by combining their "big idea" with their personal defined purpose. One of my clients combined her "big idea" of "getting America healthy with a healthy body, a healthy mind, and healthy finances" with her personal defined purpose, into a business purpose of "coaching people to help them find the motivation to take action to better themselves." She has made great breakthroughs by working on her entire purpose first business model.

When you have a purpose for your business, everything you do can be evaluated against it to see if you should pursue it.

You also need to define what success means for your business. Many businesses believe success is strictly financial, but I believe there is much more. You can define other ways you feel successful in your business when you have a defined personal purpose and a defined business purpose.

The Purpose of Purpose

Chapter 13

Creating Purpose First
Communities and Why they Matter

What about the communities you are involved in? Do they have a purpose?

Does your book group have a purpose? Does the non-profit that you volunteer for have a defined purpose? Does your PTA group have a purpose for their chapter, or do they depend upon a national statement? Does your church have a defined purpose? What about the car club you belong to? What about where you hang out and socialize with others? Do you have a purpose for participating in social media groups? What about meetups?

You need to consider the impact each different community has on you personally, and the impact you personally have on the community.

If you are involved with communities that do not have a defined purpose or have a very weak defined purpose, how are you to evaluate if your time is being well spent?

Some communities have an inherent purpose. Take religious congregations for example, where you can receive a lot of benefits from the association with others and the building up of the community.

But what about the car club or the PTA? If they do not have a defined purpose for your local group, how do you know what they stand for? Do you know if the people in the car club have ulterior motives for you being there? What about the PTA group? Are they there to help the children or are they just a gossip group that can cause trouble for just about anyone?

When you have your personal purpose defined, you can evaluate each opportunity separately. For me, if I were to join the PTA where my children go to school, I would want to know what they stood for before I committed my time and money to their organization. I happen to know the local PTA really does have their act together, so I can support them.

Creating a Defined Purpose for a Community

How do you go about creating a defined purpose for a community? It is different than a business or a job. They are usually run by volunteers with no financial interests. You must turn to people's hearts and discover what they want from the community.

First, I would sit down with all the key people who are involved and have a brainstorming session. In that session,

I would ask questions to get the group talking. Here are a few suggestions:

1. Why do we have this community?
2. What are the things we want to accomplish with this community?
3. How do each of you define success for this community?
4. What do you think are the top three things you want to accomplish with this community?
5. What is this community's "big idea"?
6. What is your (each key person) personal defined purpose?
7. How do you feel your defined purpose works with the "big idea"?

Once you get a good set of ideas, you can work though the rest of the process as it is presented in Chapter 5 of this book.

Not every community you associate with needs to have a defined purpose. But the ones that you commit a fair amount of time to are good candidates for this process.

If you work for or own a nonprofit, this process is absolutely critical for your success. If you do not have a strong defined purpose, how will the community or organization survive?

The impact of a strong defined purpose for a community could be dramatic. You can change people's lives by providing them something they can grasp on to and become passionate about. After all, isn't that what a community is really about, helping people reach out to each other to find support and comradery?

Chapter 14

What Affect Your Purpose has
on those Around You

When you started this book, what did you think you would find? When you read the title: "The Purpose of Purpose" did it make you stop for a moment and think?

I believe that the purpose of purpose is to love one another with all your heart and to give all you have to building up each other.

Every instance around the world where people are passionate about what they do for good, can be traced back to that statement. It is the key to living a joyful life and finding harmony one with another.

So what about you? What are your intentions? What do you want to do with this knowledge? Will people believe you if you state that you have found your purpose in life?

Here is where things start to get really interesting. When you have a defined purpose, people will notice that there is something different about you. They will not be able to put their finger on it, but they will know that something has changed.

Is that a good thing? Yes.

Does it make life better? Yes.

Is it easy to explain? Yes.

Is it an opening to help others discover and define their own purpose in life? Yes.

That is a responsibility I believe we all have. In fact, it is one of the main reasons I am writing this book. We have a human obligation to help each other.

You have a decision to make. What is it that you are going to do with this information? Do you want to keep it to yourself or do you want to share it with others? Since our human nature is to help other people, how can you do that? How can you show someone what you have that will make a difference in their life?

First, you can commit to making your life a purpose first life. By going through the steps I have outlined in this book, you can truly find your purpose.

Once you have found your purpose, you can share it through any means you have. When you learn something new, teaching it is the way to ingrain it into your being. Until you have your defined purpose memorized, you need to keep it where you can refer to it often. You can send it in a text message to yourself, email it to yourself, or even write it on a piece of paper and put it in your pocket.

When someone asks you how you have changed, you can simply say: "I was able to define my purpose in life, and it has made all the difference in the world to me" or something close to it.

Here is where I want to challenge you. When you define your purpose, take it to others. Take it to social media and create groups to help others find it. Let's create a worldwide movement to shift as many people as possible to a purpose first life.

Create Facebook groups, Instagram motivational groups, or send your purpose to the world in a Snapchat. Blog about it and email about it to celebrate your freedom of knowing what your purpose is.

Share your thoughts with me and others and we can create real change in the world.

What if we were able to help affect change in families, what would the chain reaction be? If we helped families overcome differences and saved marriages from ending, how would that affect the children in each of those homes?

What if we were able to affect change in communities? How could helping more people understand their purpose for being on this planet help them change? Can we even measure the potential impact that this would have in our local neighborhoods, shelters, community centers, and churches?

What if we were able to affect change for people who hold down jobs? If we were able to help increase happiness in the workplace, what difference would that make in each business, how many people would it affect for good, and how much happier would we be when we came home from work?

What if we were able to affect change for business owners and entrepreneurs? Businesses with a defined purpose can change so many things, including customer happiness which leads to employee happiness which leads to happiness when you go home from work which leads to happiness with your spouse which leads to happiness with your children.

When we find a way to live a purpose-filled life and help others find their purpose, we are at the beginning of a movement that can go through your family, friends, communities, and even throughout the world.

What if we were even able to get your local, state, and federal government to work from a purpose standpoint? If they work with a purpose, people will see it.

Above all, I want to see you smile. That is what my purpose is. I hope that these ideas will help you move in a purpose first direction.

Chapter 15

Give Yourself a
Purpose First Reality Check

What do you need to do to make your life a solid purpose first life? Basically, you need to give yourself a reality check.

What does that mean? You need to evaluate how you are doing and make any course corrections along the way.

You need to set up a "Strategic Action System" for your life. So here we go.

Define the Outcome of Your Life

What is the desired outcome of your life? What do you want to accomplish? What will it take for you to consider your life a success? This should make you think a bit. I am asking you to figure out what you consider a successful life for yourself to be.

Do not be shy. Shoot for the stars. You may have many different parts of this outcome. Part of it may be family relationships. It can be financially related. It can also include friendships, loved ones, community work, service, or a myriad of other things.

The bottom line is that it is up to you. That's right. Your definition of success is up to you. No one else's opinion matters. Only you can decide what will really make you happy at the end of your life.

Since you have already defined your purpose, you may want to consult it. You have already taken the time to list hundreds of memories from your past that have made you happy. Maybe it will give you a clue of what you would consider success for your life.

Definition of Success

_____

_____

_____

_____

_____

Define Your Purpose

Write out your purpose here:

_____

_____

_____

_____

_____

Define How

How are you going to live your life to make your out-come a reality? What choices are you going to make to bring about the success you want to achieve? What will you do to make your life a life of purpose to bring about your definition of success? What are your plans or tactics for living a happy life?

_____

_____

_____

_____

_____

_____

_____

_____

_____

_____

Constant Evaluation

How are you going to keep yourself on track? What are you going to do to find out if you are on track to reach success on your terms?

Your life's successful outcome is predicated on knowing your purpose in life. If you make a wholesale shift in your direction, start this process over.

What is your process? Will you check in with yourself weekly, monthly, yearly, or all of the above?

Define Your Process

_____

_____

_____

_____

_____

_____

_____

_____

_____

_____

_____

Chapter 16

Conclusion

Do you get it yet? Do you understand that you are the only one who has agency or free will for yourself? You have the ability to decide what your life will be like and how you will live it. All of us will have curve balls thrown our way.

We will all have challenges that will throw us off track. It could be a health issue, a financial issue, a relationship issue, or any one of a number of other things.

But if you have identified what your purpose is here on this planet, if you have identified what success will mean for you at the end of your life, how you want to live your life, how you want to help others to live a good life, and how to basically be a good person, the sky is the limit and you will have given yourself all the opportunities you could ask for.

Please, share with me your stories, your successes, your challenges, your breakthroughs, and any other experience you may have. My contact information is in the front of this book and I am looking forward to learning how this book has helped you with your personal life, professional life, and community involvement.

Once again, my purpose is: "I thrive when I look at someone smile and know that I contributed to it." I hope this book has helped bring a smile to your soul and help you live a purpose first life.

With love and in purpose,
Rod McKenzie, Jr.

Notes

Notes

Notes

Notes

www.ingramcontent.com/pod-product-compliance
Lightning Source LLC
Chambersburg PA
CBHW061958040426
42447CB00010B/1810